Turning Point

by

J. LEHMAN

DEDICATION

To all those who have read my books and students that have written to thank me years later. Oh, wait a minute, there were never any. Oh well, I'll just plug on.

CONTENTS

Dedication

1 Jane's Mouse 1

2 Ex Girl Friends 3

3 The Girl Who Washed Her Hands 7

4 Sleeping with my Ex Wife 15

5 Love Walked In 23

6 Joan Baez 29

7 Rosebud 33

8 Pretending to be a Writer 35

9 Platform 43

Author

TURNING POINT

CHAPTER 1: JANE'S MOUSE

Jane was an attractive young girl, who lived with her parents behind her grandmother's house in the Upper Peninsula. Each year there would be visitors to the summer cottage area. As a boy, I was one of them. My parents were originally from the town, but had left to go to Chicago. Now we were back.

As young children, Janeand I played together in the sand pile. As adolescents...

I would leave the house around ten. Say something about taking a walk before going to sleep and double back over to Jane's full size playhouse.

Her grandfather had built it for her when she was a young girl. It stood in the little courtyard, off in the dark, from a five-car garage this man had converted into a one-story house for his daughter, her husband, their child.

Now Jane slept in the small house.

I would approach it from the other side. Sit on one of the benches on the cement slab in front of it and talk with Janethrough the screened window. During the day you could see the words her grandfather had scraped into the wet cement. He had intended to write "Pate's House" but the "H" turned out more of an "M" so it became "Jame's Mouse."

"I don't know if I'm going to go to college," her voice came through the screen.

I waited in the dark.

"My parents would probably pay my tuition and I could save some money, living in a dormitory. Maybe be a lifeguard at the beach summers. How about you? What's going on at school for you that's exciting."

I thought. "Well we have this English teacher who makes us write for 15 minutes every day. It can be on any subject and he doesn't collect them or anything. Maybe once every couple weeks we exchange what we've written with the guy next to us (it was a Jesuit, all-boys school) and then we have to answer questions about it like, What and why are you seeing a particular image? What else does this remind you of? What was going on during this period that might have had something to do with the memory?"

"Weird!"

"Yeah," I said. "Weird." And then I walked home.

Jane's parents knew or pretended to know little about her life with friends. They were neither strict nor lenient with her.

And I? I went to mass on Sundays. Took Communion. If my parents talked about drugs or promiscuity among young people, I turned to them with an innocent face. But they didn't, just as Janenever went to college.

However, this was a time when America was giving way to passion.

One night, after a long conversation, Jane said to me, "Why don't you come in?"

She wore a silk slip. No panties. I pulled my hard penis out from my jeans and we went at it on a small bed her grandfather had made.

Jane went on to love from one day to the next, blinding herself to the years ahead, until hope was tired legs.

But, for me, that year was the beginning of the sixties with its smoke and burned grass. The sixties, And I entered them that night, through Jane's mouse.

CHAPTER 2: EX-GIRL FRIENDS

It was a small bungalow on Sherman Ave that Don shared with some other guy, Mike.

They were having a party, or I should say Don was. It was his turn and I was invited, the only guy, because I was newly hired at the restaurant where Don was manager. The rest were girls, to be exact ex-girlfriends of Don. They would soon figure this out.

Don was cooking hamburgers on a grill.

"Say, I was talking with one of the other women," said Donna who was helping him. "And she said you two were going out together ten months ago—that would have been when we broke up."

Don looked at her. She stopped putting burgers on plates.

"Well," he finally said, "the magic had gone out of our relationship. It didn' last with Karen either, in fact a few months later I started to go with Carol."

"The tall, good looking blonde in the kitchen?"

"Yes."

Once they all figured out why they had been invited, they didn't mix and left as soon as they could after dinner was served.

Don was a thirty-something, energetic, always getting glasses of water for people in the restaurant. Short, dark-haired, thin-bodied, eyebrows on the move. He finally married, Beth, a woman who trained a retarded boy to wash dishes in the kitchen.

I was grey-haired, forty, my first wife and I had moved from Michigan to Madison. I needed to find a job and wait for my teaching certificate, which would arrive in about six weeks.

I would look busy at the restaurant host-podium while secretly I wrote poems on the second shelf below where customers and Don would never see them.

Now, years later, I think of of my ex-girlfriends.

Anna had worked for me a year then quit to go to a more legitimate, higher paying job. She was fired a month later and drew unemployment I had to pay. I was angry she left and disputed the amount she got from me.

A couple years later, my second wife left and I called Anna to apologize.

We met for lunch three days later. We exchanged books by each other's favorite poets. She liked Emily Dickinson, of course, and Plath. I gave her an anthology I had of poetry and short stories by Richard Brautigan. Suddenly it became very personal.

"There's an old proverb that says cats have nine lives," I offered matter of factly. "Three to play, three to stay and three to stray."

She looked down at our chicken and cheese quesadillas and didn't say anything, but I detected the slightest hint of a smile.

Annna was single, in her forties, and now marketing director for the Madison Symphony. She had had several serious relationships, but, discarded by her last boyfriend, she was willing to share her frustration with a man twenty years older. I had suffered some disillusionment too.

I had offered to make dinner at her little Eastside bungalow one evening—salmon on angel-hair noodles with Alfredo sauce. She had not liked salmon so I ate her piece as well. Now we were sitting on her couch sipping champagne and listening to the overture from Rossini's *The Barber of Seville*. Through the front windows, I saw the high school across the street. There were no lights on and the hulking building was ominously dark.

"Nothing ever turns out for me," she finally said, on the verge of tears. "And what's worse, no one even cares."

Years ago I would have had a dozen closes to work on Anna. But now…now. Something from Kafka.

"You need an axe, right? Someone who can break up the frozen sea within you."

Her head snapped toward me. She gazed into my eyes in a whole new way, then threw her arms around my neck and tears started flowing down her alabaster cheeks.

CHAPTER 3: THE GIRL WHO WASHED HER HANDS

I suppose everyone has a double. Jack Lehrer was not mine. But we had been in many of the same classes in college and because my name came right before his when roll was called, I was aware of him, as he was of me. Then last year I took a job with a software company and the first week was sent to a trade show in Houston with their other salesperson. Surprise, it was Jack Lehrer.

After we set up the booth, we headed out for dinner. He filled me in on the company from his perspective and we traded memories from our university days. We had had a few drinks while waiting for a table in a fancy steak joint, so after the meal it was nice to settle back in our chairs and sip a little coffee. In passing, Jack had alluded to his divorce a few years earlier. Since my married life was not going well at the time, I was curious what it was like for someone my age to be single again.

I asked him whether there was a woman in his life. He thought about this for a minute, then he made a cryptic remark. I thought, perhaps he hadn't heard my question, so I said, "Have you been seeing other women since your divorce?"

Jack was a big guy, balding but with a slow, winning smile. He said, "I'll tell you, just this year I've had several, well, very unusual encounters with women."

"Come on," I said, "we've got a whole night to kill. Let's hear some details—if you want to talk about it, that is."

"Let me tell you about one of them," he said. "In fact maybe it's a good idea to talk about this with someone."

He began, "It was a few years after college. I went on to get a teaching certificate and found myself with a position as an English teacher in a poor high school in Michigan. Most of the kids had no interest in classes, but I did have one student who was not only cute but very bright. My ex-wife and I even got to know her parents. They were old-fashioned radicals from the Forties, and this, as you may know, is a very conservative, fundamentalist area. Frank was a rugged guy and Beth, the mother, a strange woman who seemed to have some kind of fixation about her father."

He laughed, and I did too. Somehow the idea of talking revolutionary politics at a backyard picnic table in the heart of Dutch Reform Church Michigan was funny.

He said, "Mary Jo also had an older sister, Jeannie. She was smart too, but psychologically troubled, even at that young age.

"Those were happy times for me," Jack sighed. "My wife and I had our first house, a little bungalow a block or so from the lake. The first years of teaching were demanding, but the summers were free. Then it was back to full days of classes, and evenings and weekends correcting papers." Jack paused. He didn't want to get lost in too much detail but needed to tell me enough to appreciate his story.

"Anyway, one day," he continued, "Beth, this student's mother, stopped at the school late in the afternoon. She was a small woman with very short, cropped hair and a face like a coconut. She asked to come into my classroom and she shut the door behind her. I had no idea what this was about, but I pulled a couple of student desks around so they faced each other and motioned for her to sit down. Without further introduction, she said, 'I have a terrible, family secret to tell you.' "

"Interesting," I found myself responding, while Jack took another drink of coffee. "What was her secret?" I was immediately a little embarrassed. Here I was asking him to reveal a personal part of this woman's life just to satisfy my passing curiosity.

But he was even more embarrassed by the question than I. His face reddened slightly and he lowered his eyes.

"I don't know," he said.

"Don't know?" I replied.

"She bent forward in the desk toward me, speaking in such hushed tones. So much so that I couldn't understand what she was saying. You've done that, haven't you? Pretended to hear or be interested in order to be polite?"

I admitted that I had.

"Later, I thought, perhaps, she'd said she was suicidal or that she had been molested by her father. But at the time my first thought was that this didn't have anything to do with the girls. My next one was, why is this woman telling this to *me*?"

Jack settled back in his chair. The restaurant was clearing out. Couples were heading back to their houses to take baby sitters home, flip on the TV for the late news or cuddle up in bed together before falling asleep. He continued, "I just wanted this strange woman out of my classroom so I could go home and get on with my life. Of course, I acted concerned and was consoling. But whether or not I had some kind of mental block to what she was saying or I honestly didn't hear the words she spoke, I had no idea what her family problem was."

Jack thought for a moment, then began again. He was now

thinking of the two girls.

"Jeannie had a weird boyfriend but she received good grades and graduated to go on to college. Mary Jo blossomed, too. She was a straight 'A' student, a top vocalist, had poems published in literary magazines—and remember she was only a high school student—starred in school plays, was an active environmental organizer, etc., etc. But no boyfriends! Even though she had naturally blonde hair and a wonderful smile. A wonderful, seductive smile. Actually, boys were intimidated by her because she was so far beyond anyone else her age in accomplishments. I'll admit, to me she was more like an interesting peer than a student. But at that time I didn't allow myself to think if it was anything other than that.

"Senior year, Mary Jo

 suddenly gave up everything for religion. Some kind of charismatic Christianity. She was living like a bible-story virgin who had delivered herself over entirely to God. She got a full scholarship to the University of Chicago to study theology and that was the last I saw of her until this year. She was eighteen when I was her teacher and now many years later, she was thirty-six. Of course I was old enough to be her father, but when she telephoned I was still trying to come to terms with my divorce, and to hear this warm, familiar voice … well, I was very pleased."

Jack remembered something and added, "I forgot to say that I'd heard she had a nervous breakdown that first year at the University. A student who was a photographer for the yearbook—I was the adviser—had a brother who worked in a mental institution. Mary Jo was taken there after the breakdown. The brother said she couldn't stop washing her hands. Two hundred, three hundred times a day she would wash her hands. The other thing I learned, and I don't remember how, was that Frank, the father, was not really the girls' father. He had married the mother when she already had the two young children."

I asked, "So, are you saying that the girls could have been parented by who? By the mother's father? Was that her secret?"

Jack looked at me and replied, "John, have you ever thought about the past. Not so much the events that happened in the past, but how we relive them through the present?"

"What do you mean?" I asked.

"Well, I guess that depends. Can we re-create ourselves like all the motivational sales books and tapes lead us to believe? Or is it fate? Are we doomed to always repeat the past in some superficially different form?"

I thought about that for a moment, about my marriage that had once seemed happy enough, but now wasn't. Was I looking for something new or trying to find something that I'd had in the past that would fall apart all over again? I thought about my daughter, now an adult. To me she seemed both a woman and the emotional child she had always been.

Jack continued, "Whether the past is a treasure worth reclaiming or some kind of stigma that marks us and turns ordinary things we do into penance, it's always there, isn't it? And sometimes it surfaces as unexpectedly as a phone call. A phone call in the middle of the night from Chicago."

"Mary Jo?" I asked.

"Yes," he said. She called out of nowhere late one night. She had found my name through an Internet search. I didn't even have to time to turn on the lights and there, over the receiver, was her voice in the dark, coming out of the past.

"I pictured those thin arms and white hands, her full mouth and blonde hair. I could smell Lake Michigan and feel the trudge of walking in the sandy, lake shore dunes. It had been almost twenty years since we'd packed up the kids and left Michigan for a new life in Wisconsin. A life of frustration and financial hardship that had ultimately driven us apart. But now, in the sound of Mary Jo's voice, there was a promise bubbling up like an underground spring.

"Mary Jo and I talked for an hour and a half. Her parents, Elsie and Frank, had died five years earlier within months of each other. Her sister, Jeannie, had not married her boyfriend but a rather conservative businessman. She'd been on medication for depression, but last summer decided not to take it anymore. Like Virginia Woolf, one night she walked out into Duck Lake until she drowned. Now Mary Jo Briggs—`Briggs' was her married name— was alone except for her husband of a year. He too had left her but then he came back, she said, providing she agreed to `certain conditions.'

"Anyway, she wanted to see me ... had to see me. She wondered if that would be possible. As it turned out, I needed to schedule a business trip to Chicago within the next two weeks. I told her I would call the following day after I had pinned down the date.

But something was strange right from the start," Jack said. By now, we were the only ones left in the restaurant and the staff were starting to do their clean up tasks.

"What?" I asked.

"Well," he replied. "When I called her the next night, she

said, `Hello.' I gave my name, but when I started to talk about what day I would be in Chicago, without saying a further word, she suddenly hung up."

"Hung up?"

"Yes, I called again thinking that I might have dialed the wrong number, but the same thing happened the second time."

"That was peculiar," I said.

"Yes, but you haven't heard anything yet," he replied.

"What do you mean?"

"She phoned the next morning with absolutely no explanation for what had happened the night before, instead telling me in a breathy, beseeching voice that she'd be overjoyed to meet me. So we set up a time and place. Though when I hung up the phone, I had a rather unsettled feeling."

Back at the hotel, Jack continued his story. We sat in a corner of the Hilton's two-story lobby. There was a small bar and we each ordered a brandy. Many miles from home in a strange place, we huddled together before a gas fire of fake logs that didn't burn.

I realized just how much I enjoyed Jack. He was proving to be a more interesting and sensitive guy than I'd remembered. And, a youthful face beneath his own seemed to light up as he talked about his anticipation over this meeting with a woman who'd been a former student he obviously had been infatuated with. A chance to make good on an unfulfilled promise. Wasn't that what I wanted? Though his experiences were different from mine, they were somewhat parallel. It was almost as if we were each playing chess with some unseen opponent, except he was a couple moves ahead of me in his game. I was anxious to see if what happened to him could apply to my life.

"I arrived in the Old Town section of Chicago, where we were to meet, about an hour early," Jack said. "I thought I'd have trouble finding parking, but as it turned out there was a spot just behind the restaurant. It was a warm late-afternoon in June and I sat at a table outside."

"Having some beer?" I asked him.

"I have to admit I did have a few beers while I waited," he said. "I had grown up in Chicago and the afternoon was awash with memories. As a kid I'd taken the el to this part of town and explored its shops and coffee houses. During my college breaks I'd make a point of hitting one of the clubs to catch a folk music act and maybe get a little drunk. And now, here I was again at another stage in my life."

"So what happened?" I asked.

"Listen," he said. "you've got to believe me, I'll try to be as exact as I can."

He took a drink of water to clear his throat.

"The meeting lasted less than a minute. What I remember most is mumbling some lame excuse, then walking, almost at a run, through the restaurant, past the kitchen and out the door to my car parked in back."

"What do you mean?" I asked, trying to make sense out of what he was saying. "I'm not following you. You were at the restaurant, and then what?"

Jack said, "I was sitting at that outdoor table looking down the street when I heard a voice. It came from the sidewalk behind my back. It said, 'Mr. Lehrer?'

"I turned slowly not knowing what to expect. It had been so many years since I'd last seen Mary Jo but I still half thought that she would look the same. She stood right in front of the setting sun and I was blinded by it. I could only make out the shape of her body and her golden hair. The blonde around her face was glowing like a rim of sun around the moon in an eclipse."

Jack stared at me. Then, almost in a whisper, said: "When she came forward, as her face bent down toward mine out of that halo of sun, I saw that it was not her face at all, but the shriveled, coconut-like face of her mother ..."

Jack was lost in the shock of that moment.

"And," he finally continued, "from the pressed lips of that face I heard a distant voice. It said, '... I want my secret back.' "

I looked at Jack. We were lost in the vast night doomed by our mistakes. I could feel the board tilting, the imaginary chess pieces plummet toward the ground.

CHAPTER 4: SLEEPING WITH MY EX WIFE

Now they wanted to have sex together. Pamela was fifteen; William was fifteen. They had been neighbors and close friends since grade school. It would be the first time for each of them.

Perhaps they didn't both want it in the same way. Pamela, with her come-hither smile, chestnut ponytail and incessant pirouetting was my daughter. Her mother and I had been married for twenty years; now we were divorced. Pat lived in our old home on the East Side of Madison while I rented a duplex across from the Arboretum on the West Side. My daughter made a list each morning and at the end of the week consolidated what she hasn't accomplished into a weekly list. Then monthly, then yearly. I could almost see "Have sex with William" on one of these, which perhaps she shared with her mother. And her mother, a caterer by profession, would have said, "Let's just see if we can't arrange it."

Pamela spent two days a week with me. This was a happy arrangement since, if the family were still together, I probably would have been excluded from any and all of her teenage doings. Now I was an active participant, particularly since she proved adept at pitting her mother and me against one another.

"Dad, I need a queen sized futon with a comfy quilt like the one I have at Mom's."

"Sure, Hon, in fact why don't we go to the Furniture

Loft and maybe get you a new dresser too."

"And a mirror with the New York skyline and a chrome lamp, the kind that has lots of colored shades?"

"We'll see." And that teak dining room table and set of chairs, I thought. All I had to do is to fill out the form for another credit card.

I'd already spent over $4,000 that I didn't have on furnishings as compensation to my daughter and myself for the divorce. But I had not had much choice. I had rented my duplex without actually seeing its interior. How bad could it be with such a picturesque location, you ask? Well, it was like one of those cardboard mousetraps—a door on each side, sticky floors and no side windows.

I went for a Japanese, minimal look with bare wood floors, rice mats and fat scented candles. As anyone over the age of eight who has tried to watch TV sitting on the floor knows, this has its drawbacks.

But I loved wandering the trails in the Arboretum across the street at night. It was like entering a woodcut of a Brothers Grimm forest. And when the pale moon rose through outstretched branches, and I knew no one else was around, I'd lean back and howl like a wolf, and let all the frustration and hurt I felt—all the loneliness, all the fear— bellow out. Sometimes, afterwards I'd curl up on a bed of old leaves and cry.

"Hello, John, this is Pat, your ex-wife." She waved that designation like a Civil War platoon emerging from battle flourishing its Stars and Bars. How many Pats do I know, for godsake? Did she expect me to say, "Oh, *that* Pat?"

"Listen, I've arranged for Pamela and William to have their first intimate sexual experience together this Friday. They will have a romantic dinner here at the house and later go up to our old bed and spend the night."

"OK?"

"I've talked this over with William's mother and have reviewed the use of condoms with Pamela."

I didn't know what to say. It was like the time I got bit by a stray dog parking my car behind the duplex late one night. I grunted.

"And I will spend the night at your place…sleeping with you."

The old and the new. There it was, I thought. The first tentative intimacy between young lovers and a fling in the dark for two disillusioned old ones. But like William, I was a guy. Guys don't have "sex" on a list with ten other things. If there is a list at all—and there isn't—sex is the only thing on it. In bold, boxy letters with no frilly squiggles or stars or hearts. Just "SEX."

The first time I had sex with Pat was when I was stationed in Heidelberg, Germany. She had been a tourist traveling with friends when she decided to stay and took a job at the hospital where I was an administrator. We'd done a few lunch and drive-in-the-hills kinds of things but she had earned enough money to take off for Paris and no one was going to interfere with that.

Several weeks later I had a phone call one evening at the bachelor officers' quarters where I lived. She said she was driving from Switzerland where she'd had a bad experience—someone had tried to rape her—and wondered if she could come stay with me.

She arrived about four in the morning, piled her backpack and sleeping bag just inside my front door and gave me a trembling, death-grip of a hug.

"How ya doing?" I asked standing in my boxer shorts.

"I drove straight through. I just want to be here…with you." This last phrase she slyly added as she glanced at my cotton underpants tenting out.

The next thing I remember, I was lying naked on my single, army-issue bed. What excited me most when she came in nude from the bathroom was her bush of public hair. Pat was short and bosomy in a Miss Piggy sort of way, but when she straddled me, there was a determined look in her eyes—her hair tossed back in a sweat, some of it sticking to the sides of her face. She wore green eyeliner and the lids of her eyes, when she closed them, were black. I was too intimidated to climax. I did when we went at it again the following morning after a night of twisted, sexual dreams.

She stayed with me for twenty years after I left the service. I thought that was love. Ah, William, we men have a lot to learn!

Now it was around 9 pm. I had decided to forgo any "romantic dinner" and was just slicing some Brie and opening a cheap bottle of Merlot when the doorbell rang.

On my way to opening the front door, I restarted the Sinatra CD ("The Tender Trap") and threw some dark socks lying in the middle of the room under one of the two chrome, Breuer chairs.

At first I though it was someone else. The last time I had seen Pat was when I went to give her my set of keys to our house. I remembered standing on the front porch—"our front porch"—ringing the bell. No one answered. Through the bay window I could see there was a fire in the fireplace (this was still early spring) and women in what looked like dressy gowns sipping champagne or wine. Their dresses sparkled in the light of the dancing flames. I tapped on the glass and someone inside squealed, "A man."

Presently Pat had come to the door. She stepped out onto the porch, closing the door behind her.

"I'm having a small gathering of friends," she explained.

There was something pathetic about my being shut out of my own house that must have shown on my face, for she was surprisingly tender.

"Thanks for bringing the keys over. We'll talk. Soon. Okay? We'll talk."

Her hair, just starting to grey, was worn up on her

head—probably to make her look taller. She had on a soft, velvet dress sprinkled with sequins. There was a subtle hint of liner and eye shadow, which she had not worn since our daughter, was born.

Tonight when I opened the door, not only were the severe bangs and shoulder length black hair back, but the full, outlandish eye make-up. Her once-freckled skin was cold-cream white. She was anorexia thin. AND—listen, I know this is hard to believe—she was taller than she had ever been.

But, it was Pat all right. She brushed past me did a quick inspection of my *fen-shui* living/dining area then disappeared into the kitchen. The next thing I knew she was coming down from the bedrooms upstairs (how had she gotten up there?).

"This is okay, Jack. You have done well for yourself."

"How 'bout a glass of wine," was all I could reply.

And so we sat and talked.

We were almost through the bottle of wine when she came over, took my hand and started to lead me up toward my bedroom. Whether we had talked about our daughter's evening, life since the divorce or how lush the scented mid-summer air felt blowing in through the screens, I can't remember. All I recall is blowing out all but one of the candles, which I took with us, leaving the first floor of the duplex in darkness.

We climbed the shadowy, wooden staircase, and just

as she had done a little over twenty years ago, when we reached the top she disappeared into the bathroom.

I put the candle on the bedside table and shucked my clothes. When she came in, she was naked, carrying a small bottle. I propped myself up on my elbows and started to say something.

"Shhhhhh," she purred kneeling next to me on the futon.

I leaned back and felt a stream of scented oil on my genitals. Before long she was kneading them in her hands. I slipped my hand between her legs and started to massage her labia with my fingers. Then the bouncing, battering main event began.

While Pamela and William were fumbling at intercourse for the first time, her parents were locked in the combat to which it leads. It wasn't love.

Pat bucked on top of me rodeo style. She moaned and, at one point, even shrieked. I arched my back to provide a brass pole for this ghoulish whore to gyrate on.

After we were done, Pat fell into a cavernous sleep. I was wide-awake. Everything in my life had been ruined. Someone must pay. That's when I looked closely at her face in the glow of the candle. There was something very strange about it. Her teeth. Pat's jaw hung slightly open (she breathed through her mouth when she slept) and I saw that her incisors were considerably longer than they should have been.

What the hell! I quickly blew out the candle.

That's when it hit me. I recalled the baroque gathering of women at our house that I had stumbled upon—the blazing fire, formal gowns, flowing champagne. I lay back on my pillow. The irony of the situation was not that she had literally become a vampire but that I was not even worth her bite.

Perhaps my daughter was also a vampire. Maybe this was the real reason they had invited William to spend the night. He was to be a young prince joining the clan of the damned. He, not I, merited immortality.

I raised my right hand to my nose and sniffed the smell of her vagina still on my thumb and forefinger. Then I rose up on my hands and knees. I was a naked figure crouching over her, just as thirty minutes ago she had knelt over me.

Bored by the prospect of me as a victim, my ex-wife had fallen asleep. But we both had changed. She hadn't seen the congealing clouds in the window dramatically part and the yellow orb of a moon peek through. She'd missed something else too. How my ears extended. How a carpet of hair covered my body. The way saw-like teeth now crowded my lupine jaw.

Divorce had changed us both. Pat was a vampire and I...I had become a werewolf. A werewolf who'd missed dinner. Luckily there was a caterer handy. For I was hungry. Very, very hungry.

CHAPTER 5: LOVE WALKED IN

"That's what I said, 'You're Mom and I are getting a divorce.'"

"But why? You've been married for twenty years," my daughter replied.

And I thought about that Sunday dinner my wife and I had had at the old Fess Hotel. The surprise bouquet of roses our seventeen year old, Vandana, had arranged to be delivered to the table. How, on the drive home Pat had said, maybe it would work after all. But it didn't. I thought about the two months of what I believed was marriage counseling and, after it was over, how she had revealed it was just her way of letting me down easily. How we sat on the steps outside the psychologist's building afterwords and had nothing more to say to one another.

I gave my daughter a hug. It was the end of our Saturday morning breakfast together, and said, "We both love you and Karl as our kids, and doing things as a family, but soon you will be off to college and Karl has joined the Air Force. Your mother … no both of us have to ask ourselves what we want out of the *next* twenty years and I'm afraid the answers are things we can accomplish better separately than together."

Vandana stood up, pulling herself together, and walked out to the kitchen. I began to gather the dirty dishes but by the time I'd brought them into the dishwasher she was gone.

I remembered that day outside of the marriage

counselors. The sky had been gray. I bought myself a steak to eat weeks later when I moved out. Pat would buy new sheets, a new bead spread and new pillow cases. Months passed. I also purchased a set of Teflon pots and pans. Pat would rake her garden and act in a play.

***

"So, John, why don't you tell Pat and me what it is that you want from marriage you are not getting from yours, and then we'll give Pat a turn answering the same question."

God knows I had thought this over many times before this gawky marriage counselor in khaki pants and K-Mart shirt had asked it in his non-judgmental voice. The easy answer was that I didn't want the kind of marriage my parents had had. Full of routine, polite conversation, playing solitaire across from each other every night at the kitchen table, watching TV, sleeping in separate bedrooms. It was as if they were marking off the days of a life sentence. They each had lived their own lives: he painting with oils in the basement while he listened to classical music each evening after a day at the office; she, her bridge club, the grand children. In summer she tended a rose garden in their backyard.

"I feel we are leading separate lives already," I finally had answered. "I'm trying to build a business. Pat is impatient with that."

"An ad agency, for godsake."

"Unhappy with its progress, she has become a realtor. I don't see her even nights and weekends anymore."

"You're jealous because I finally have some money. A new car."

"John, Pat, you don't have to answer each other or be defensive. We're just trying to establish how we all feel about the issue."

 Pat's black hair had whirled as she shoved her notebook into a saddle bag-like purse. She had stood up and grabbed her leather coat from the back of her chair."

"Here's how I feel," she'd said, glaring at me, all five feet of her quivering with indignity, "I'm outa here!"

It wasn't as simple as that, of course. That evening after I had told our daughter and later our son, I'd found Pat in the basement. She was sitting in a chair in the dark in the middle of a room where she made her wall hangings. It had once been a coal bin, but now the bricks were painted with a glossy enamel that seemed to shine even in the dark . She was crying. Unwilling to talk or be comforted, she sat upright in the chair, crying.

***

It was November, six months later. Vandana and I sat in Amy's café. She had started in as a student at the University of Wisconsin. There was the smell of rain-wet jackets hung along a wall rack in the cozy restaurant. Two-person tables stood in orderly rows to the left, a bar and stools on the right. Neon reflected in the mirror behind the bar.

We both ordered cheese-broccoli soup, and I, an
order of fries. A guy sitting at the bar joked with the
bartender, and at the only other occupied table two
coeds waited for their food. Vandana talked about
boys as I dumped sugar on my fries when they came,
mistaking it for salt. We were waiting for her mother,
who I'd invited, but suspected would not show up.
She never did.

Another year passed. This time I was sitting in Amy's
alone. There was no longer cigarette smoke. A man
talked on a cell phone. The outside door didn't want to
close properly. Miles Davis played on the sound
system. I drank a mid-afternoon coffee. Someone left.
I got up to shut the door, and what do you know, a tall,
short-haired woman (my future second wife) in a
hand-woven parka walked in.

CHAPTER 6: JOAN BAEZ

Then, only two years or three ago.

"My parents were hippies," Shoshauna had said. Not the young Joan Baez but someone with the same long black hair, wide eyes, distinctive nose and turned up Joan Baez lips. This was over lunch at a little cafe a mile or two from downtown Madison where she worked. It had cathedral ceilings, over-head fans and, of course, several young adults on their laptops. "I had twenty-six lovers before I got married to Harry. He was the opposite. Security and dependability I thought I needed."

All I heard was the "twenty-six lovers." After her husband I would make twenty-eighth, I had thought, I remembered now as I sat in the same café two years later and ate a barbecued beef sandwich, drank a Brazilian coffee with cream. It was a knitting shop/coffee house—a knitting shop/coffee house, only in Madison, I sighed. There were two-person tables, a couple of well-worn couches by the door, and a weaving hanging on the wall.

 I noticed an outside terrace with a wrought iron fence around it. Stepping out, I saw the Capital building and downtown Madison across the bay.

I hadn't understood Buddhism until I fell in love with a writer. We were both married to other people under an imprint of marriage from the fifties. Like a piece of writing that you think should go a certain way, but ends us something else. I had discovered that things did not have a value intrinsic in themselves, but that "good" or "bad" were labels we placed upon them to fit our perspective at the time.

The two of us had met after belonging to an on-line critique group with occasional pot-luck dinners. I had this idea of putting on a workshop/open mike at a bookstore in Baraboo, Wisconsin. I could have done it myself but thought it might prove more interesting to have two poets do it—a man and a woman.

As I watched her standing at the book store microphone between the woman reading poems her son had written about his father's suicide and an old lady who had reduced her life to rhyming aphorisms…as I listened to her voice, a married woman's evoking scenes of unrequited love like those in a mountain ballad sung by Joan Baez when I was a teen, I realized I was in love with her.

Her eyes, nose and a chin that quivered a bit with uncertainty. Would she let me take her in my arms or hold her ground. Outside during the intermission, the air was chilly. There were hints of snow. Neither of us moved. Her eyes widened. Suddenly, I knew.

Later, between the shelves of fiction and nonfiction, I grabbed her to me and kissed her.

She was like a Saudi woman he had only seen parts of. Lidded eyes, the flick of a white wrist, the angle of her neck. Images that still haunt me years later as I slid down a shaft to the bottom of sleep that became doves filling morning air when I awoke. She was always there. A ghost on the periphery. An infidel to the ordinary. Back then I knew Imust keep channels open. Be ready and waiting for her when she chose to appear.

In the coffee house that long-ago afternoon, there was nothing dividing us from everything that is. The Buddhists say, "without a past there is no guilt. Without the future, no fear." Her look had implied they could pretend whatever they wanted. I had sipped from my earthen mug. We'd sat. Breathed. We held each other in our eyes.

Without guilt and fear who were we? Me and her.

On her birthday, I leaned over her and held her head in my hands. She turned her face to the side, offering a cheek for my kiss. Her eyes closed and she rested a hand on my shoulder, kneeling on a lush meadow that dropped to a precipice behind her. Her black hair blossomed with flowers like small butterflies though her bare feet, braced against the edge, were garlanded in gold chains.

"Will there be anything else?" the matronly waitress asked me, impatient to clear the table.

That, I thought, was the question.

Off of Atwood Avenue, across from Olbrich Botanical Gardens, the grounds of Olbrich Park are expansive and beautiful, lining the shores of Lake Monona. While a tots soccer game and an adult soccer game simultaneously played on the fields, the two of us sat at a picnic table by the water under a tree with fiery October leaves. Cribbage, mimosas, and later an ice cream sandwich from the ice cream truck in the parking lot—a very good Saturday. If we hadn't filled up on snacks, we probably would have had a taco or two from the taco truck that was also in the parking lot every Saturday and Sunday.

Now two years later, I wander Olbrich Gardens by himself, through a maze of gardens, to circular hubs of sculptures with bubbling water and tree-umbrellaed inlets along the creek. A sign across the bridge to the golden Thai Pavilion— that glowed like a golden treasure in the distance—says it is closed due to maintenance.

I slink into an old Adirondack chair.

We might have been lovers in Arles wandering streets not far from fields where Van Gogh went mad, I thought. She a black and white photograph taken with an old Roliflex. Me, a poet or a playwright. She would stop time. In one frame I might be holding a wedge of Camembert big as slice of cheesecake. In another, at a sidewalk café, waiving away smoke from stonemasons at the table next to our table. Our eyes might reflect vineyards at dusk as we'd sip espresso, share a dish of crepes au Grand Mariner. Above, metal balconies, just large enough for pots of red geraniums would cling to the building's pale facade. And along the lane would be a shop piled with dried herbs and spices—peppercorns mixed with tiny rosebuds to grind on roast lamb.

Suddenly in my dream of Province she would bow her head and say, "There are feelings I have, so deep I can't go there."

In real life neither of us did. Now, like the love for Joan Baez from my lonely teens, through the wrong end of a telescope, the woman seems further and further away.

But getting back to Don's party. I was like his father. In fact I think that's why he hired me. His older brother got the golf equipment business when the old man died, but with these former girls Don was trying to prove something else.

CHAPTER 7: ROSEBUD

Lost in an over-sized usher's jacket,
Burns takes my ticket then scurries
behind the snack bar just in case I,
his classmate, might want to splurge.

I walk the slanting entrance way
past posters of Gable, Stanwick
and Dean. The place will soon be
a bowling alley that also closes—

and raucous Saturday matinees
of popcorn, crawling over seats
and screaming chums become a
silent parking lot. But this Thursday

is my last chance to watch Orson
Welles in *Citizen Kane*. Back then
you went to movies when you liked
and stayed on for what you missed.

Leaving half-way through the second
showing, I see I am the only person
here. The projector stops. The screen

goes blank. I don't feel any sadness,

but more like I'm a big-shot motion

picture mogul myself, with people to

meet, places to go, deals to make,

in a golden age that will never end.

CHAPTER 8: PRETENDING TO BE A WRITER

It was the day before yesterday. I had my computer chair facing away from the computer and was putting on my socks when I managed to twirl a little and the back hit the handle of a travel mug of coffee next to my keyboard. The tipped-over cup spilled on the keyboard, went under my phone, and the coffee even formed a small, brown lake beneath my DVD player and stack of noir DVDs.

"Damn," I said to the empty room. This is why an audience want to identify with characters who commandeer someone else's life, like the musician in *Detour* or the woman in Cornel Woodrich's *I Married a Dead Man*. Ah, to be someone else. Someone who has it good. But even if you were and you dumped your morning coffee, you'd be pissed. That's what got me thinking, if we could be someone else, would we feel the same way anyhow?

You might note that I had too much time on my hands. This was due to a lack of new clients for my free-lance copyrighting business. I had been filling the days by writing short stories. Maybe that's when it dawned on me: Weren't writers recreating themselves through their characters and putting them into circumstances that, if not ideal, the writer at least controlled?

Sopping up the coffee I remembered one of the stories I had written, "The Girl Who Washed Her Hands." In it, a high school teacher going through a divorce is contacted by one of his more unusual students of ten years earlier. I used a girl I had known in my English class when we were both high school students. Mary Jo was sort of a genius, who the girls resented and, despite her blonde good looks, the boys were afraid of. In my story her mother confides some family secret to the teacher in a parent teacher conference. The teacher is courteous but a bit annoyed as the session was to focus on the student not her mother's past. I pictured the mother as having a shriveled, coconut-like head.

Now the reason I was thinking of this particular story on an overcast January, Monday morning, was that I had received an out-of-the-blue e-mail the night before from this girl I had known in high school. Why me? I remembered we once almost went on a date. I had asked her to go to an Ingmar Bergman Sunday movie matinee at an art house on the near North Side of Chicago. She'd hesitantly accepted. I even went so far as to go to the movie earlier in the week so I could prepare some things to say about it for our El ride home. Then, the day before our date, she canceled. A couple years later, the gossip that reached me in the Army from the only high school classmate I kept in touch with was that she had attended a theology program at the University of Chicago, had a nervous breakdown and had spent a few months in a mental institution where she had washed her hands 300 to 400 times a day.

As I continued to get dressed that morning—putting on yesterday's jeans, black   t-shirt and an old pull-over sweater—I thought how I'd gotten an interesting short story out of this, which had never been published, of course, but was still somewhat personally cathartic.

In any case, Mary Jo indicated that she was now moving to Madison and had looked up former, fellow students on the Internet. I was the only one located here. We would have our date after all.

One of my clients, a restaurant, had hit it big. I suggested we meet there a week from Tuesday for dinner. I knew I wouldn't have to pay for the meal.

I picked her up at the YWCA at 7pm. She obviously didn't know much about cars because she was impressed by my beat-up '78 Oldsmobile Cutlass Supreme. It was dark and the rust didn't show.

"So what have you been doing," I asked. Unlike the girl in my story she looked good since I had last seen her ten years earlier. Very good. Her hair was now a 40's platinum she wore up in a fashionable Kim Novak style. She was pencil thin but had large, large breasts that made her bend slightly forward when she walked and that ear-to-ear grin I remembered from high school.

"I have several degrees. One in pharmacy. In fact that's why I got this Madison job offer at the UW Hospital. And you?"

We parked in back of the restaurant on East Washington. I could make up stuff. In fact I knew I would, but what. I couldn't fake "several degrees" with this person. It wasn't that I cared what she thought of me, but she was just too smart for anything but the truth. I suppose I could have embroidered a bit on my copyrighting business, but that sounded "shoe-string" no matter what I'd say.

"Oh, I'm a successful short-story writer with a best-selling new collection." I said with a swagger. "Should we go in and get some dinner?" And the winner of round one: the accomplished professional advertising liar.

There were five or six wide concrete steps leading up to the arched entrance way of the restaurant. It was one of those old yellow brick buildings that looked like it could have been a railroad station, except there were no tracks nearby.

There was a podium for the host as we entered. A circular bar to the right and to the left a long narrow room with a brick floor and along the windows an assortment of old wooden tables separated from one another by shutter-like folding partitions. The overhead lights were faux candled fixtures and Vivaldi was piped in through hidden ceiling speakers.

"What's the name of your book?" she asked. Her tone sounded skeptical.

"*The Girl Who Washed Her Hands*. This, I knew, was an unfortunate choice as soon as I uttered it. But maybe she wouldn't make the connection to herself.

Suddenly there was a chill between us. An animosity, even bitterness. She had made the connection of the title to her own life.

"I'd like to see a copy of your book," she said. Her tone was accusatory.

"And I'd like you to see it. But it was published by a small imprint in California so the collection isn't readily available in bookstores here in the Midwest. They sent me some copies, but unfortunately I sent them all out to relatives. You know how it is?"

"What about amazon?"

"Not up yet. I don't know what those people are doing!" I detoured past that rather handily. "But what's been happening with you."

She smiled slyly and said nothing. Behind those penetrating grey eyes, was anybody's guess.

"My sister died recently," she finally said.

In my story the girl who met her former teacher years later, had turned into that coconut- headed mother (at least in the narrator's mind). And her chilling incantation to him was, "I want my secret back."

"I'm sorry," I said, suddenly confused.

"No, you don't understand," she said taking her fork and starting in on the broccoli quiche she had ordered. But she didn't say any more.

The waiter brought my salmon and we both ate quietly.

 "What do you mean, I don't understand," I finally broke the silence.

She sipped her glass of Zinfandel. "Just this, you Shit, I am not Mary Jo, but her sister. Mary Jo's story, which you apparently used to build your literary success, is dead."

I wanted to say that I was innocent. That my portrayal of Mary Jo was as much about the mother as anything. That I wasn't a successful author. That no one except me and a few publications I'd sent it to had ever read the story. And that is what I should have told her, but didn't. Instead, I said, "But why would you pretend to be her instead of telling me this in your e-mail?"

"You don't even want to know…how she filled the pockets of her jeans and windbreaker with rocks and walked out into Duck Lake? How can you sit there and not care?"

"Is everything all right?" the young waiter, Steve, asked taking our plates. "Would you like some desert?"

I tried to think back over my short story. Had I been sorry for the girl? Why had I written it? Were there ghosts about my own relationship with my mother that I couldn't address directly?"

"Give me the keys to your car," she commanded, pushing back from the table. "The keys!"

"No, listen I stammered, I…." But, in shock, did take my keys out of my pocket and put them on the table. Steve, not wanting to be witness to a scene, had slipped off.

"Oh, don't worry about your precious vehicle. You'll get it back."

Now the reason we were eating at this particular restaurant was, as I said, they were a client of mine. Their name was "The Washington Post," just like the newspaper. The owner hired me after they received a critical review in the local newspaper: "Food Bad, Service Worse" and gave me a small advertising budget. Those ads caught the attention of some stringers for the legendary newspaper who sent on my little display ads along with a menu bearing the name in the paper's copyrighted type script to their bosses. A massive lawsuit followed with surprising results.

The restaurant was clearly in the wrong but other media, anxious for any excuse to pick on their rival, blew this up into a modern "David versus Goliath" story. A national law firm offered to represent the restaurant *pro bono*. The owner got his name in *Time Magazine*. And there were suddenly customers. Customers. Coming to see what all the fuss was about. The Washington *Post Newspaper* backed off and I had my first real advertising success.

As I walked home by myself that night under a starry sky, past trees whose leaves were like wind chimes coated with ice. I couldn't help but wonder at it all.

There was no sign of my car, but fortunately I had hidden an extra key to my home under the back-entrance doormat.

"You own an old Oldsmobile?" the voice on the phone said the next morning.

"Yes."

"Well I'm Sergeant Mullins of the Monona Police Force and we found it this morning driven into the river at the boat launch, the keys are in it but no one's around."

I explained the incident of the night before and told them I would pick the car up from the towing company who they had pull it out of the water. But after another night's sleep, I knew something else that I didn't bother to tell them.

The reason I had so readily bought the story about her being her sister was that in my story the girl had aged. Had turned into her mother. And after I wrote that it had become the truth for me. I had believed it. And why did Mary Jo lie to me? To get her revenge. She'd been like the *Washington Post Newspaper* and felt that I, like the restaurant, had used her image for my own advantage. I had, of course. That should have been the end of the story. Except it wasn't.

There was a third element. In the case of the newspaper versus the restaurant it was the other media. In my case it was a letter I retrieved from my mailbox on my way out that morning.

It was an acceptance of "The Girl Who Washed Her Hands" by *American Short Fiction Quarterly*. Suddenly I was that writer I was pretending to be, and I felt great.

CHAPTER 9: PLATFORM

The saddest thing I remembered about my father was when my grandfather died. I was six or seven when I overheard Mom and Dad talking about the funeral. It was being held in Menomonee, Michigan where he had lived. My mother didn't want to go.

Both of my parents had lived in this UP. My mother, her two sisters and her widowed mother, packed up and moved to Chicago when the girls graduated from high school. They bought a house and the three young women went to schools for nursing, education and for banking. It was a brave thing for women to do in 1930's but these were strong. My father was not. He was recruited out of his senior high school engineering class by a Chicago firm that made draft gears—the mechanisms behind the couplers that absorbed the shock when trains stopped or cars coupled with other cars. Mom was from a family of Catholics. But my father was a non-practicing Presbyterian. In their own hometown it would have been out of the question for the two to even date. In Chicago they could do what they pleased; so they got married.

There was one major difference between them, besides religion. My father had an affection for small town life. In his heart he longed to return. My mother and her sisters were glad to leave the limitations of the rural area behind them. This was the reason behind the one she gave why she wouldn't go back for the service and my father, not one to express his feelings openly or impose his will on another, let it go at that. I don't know why I wasn't asked to accompany him, but I wasn't. What I do know was how families felt when a spouse didn't accompany their husband or wife to a parent's wake.

My mother must have driven him to the railroad station when he left, because days later, she and I drove to Union Station for his return. She checked the arrival board and then we walked down stairs to a platform   beside the track where the train was scheduled to come in. Finally the huge diesel engine, *The 400,* crawled by. To me, a small boy a train was an imposing sight. Even at slow speed there was an air of heavy inevitability about it and a sense of real occasion—a scraping sound of metal wheels on metal rails, conductors gamely hanging from windows at the end of cars, the sigh of the hydraulic breaking system and a final jolt of this mega-ton force finally coming to a halt. There were only three cars with passengers and we had picked the correct one. A conductor stood at the foot of the car's stairs, in dusty blue uniform coat and dapper, black rimmed hat,his helping hand out for a trip. And that was when my father at the top of the stairs, for a moment looked out at us,at the big city, as if in a time of need this world had let him down.Then that expression was gone, forever.

He stepped down to join us. He hugged my mother, shook my hand. For someone who didn't often express sadness and disappointment he had all the reinforcement he needed why you shouldn't show those emotions.   People—worse yet, people you loved—let you down.

ABOUT THE AUTHOR

J. Lehman is the founder and original publisher of *Rosebud*, a national magazine of short stories, poetry and illustration for people who enjoy good writing. For twenty years he was the literary editor of the *Wisconsin People & Ideas* and currently is managing partner of Zelda Wilde Publishing and editor/publisher of *Lit Noir* magazine. Lehman was a finalist for the Wisconsin Poet Laureate position in 2004 and again in 2008.

He teaches regularly at UW School of the Arts, The Loft, The Clearing, Green Lake Writers' Conference and at the UW Waukesha.

Dramatic readings of his plays, *A Brief History of My Tattoo, The Jane Test, The Writer's Cave* and *The Last Day of the Sixties* have been presented in Milwaukee, Madison, Whitewater (Wisconsin) and Saint Petersburg, Florida. His collections of poetry include *Acting Lessons, Shrine of the Tooth Fairy, Dogs Dream of Running, Shorts: 101 Brief Poems of Wonder and Surprise, To the Movies, The Village Poet and You Betcha*. His latest nonfiction books are *America's Greatest Unknown Poet: Lorine Niedecker Reminiscences, Photographs, Letters and Her Most Memorable Poems, Dancing in the Rain, The Trouble with Happiness, Without a Blindfold, Playing Chess with My Daughter* and *Everything is Changing: How to Gain Loyal Customers and Clients Quickly*. Plus, *Writing is My Religion*. All of his books are available from Amazon or www.DamnGoodBooks.com.

He grew up in Chicago but for the last twenty-five years has lived with his wife, Talia Schorr, their three dogs and ten cats in Rockdale, the smallest incorporated village in Wisconsin.

46

POETRY
(Under the name John Lehman)
Shrine of the Tooth Fairy
Dogs Dream of Running
Shorts, Brief Poems of
    Wonder and Amazement
Acting Lessons
The Village Poet
To the Movies
You Betcha

FICTION
Geography of Sleep
Man with One Ear
Wolves beneath Chicago
Lit Noir
Men without Meaning
Tales Told in the Dark
Shadows of Unseen Things
Goddess of Unspeakable Things
Lost on Clearview Road
Please Adjust Your Mask
Waiting for Dharma
The Angry Grandfather Chronicles
Not For You Kids
Downward Facing Dog
The All-Night Mystery Story
Sophie Tucker Speaks
The Big Metaphor
The Shadow Knows
Dogs That See Ghosts

NON-FICTION
Writing Magic
Short Story Magic
Autobiography Magic
Write On
Turning Points
America's Greatest Unknown

Poet: Lorine Niedecker
Everything is Changing: How to
    Gain Loyal Clients and Customers
Write Angles
Write What You'd Love To Read
The Bark of Love
How and Why a Poem Works
Around Midnight: How to Write a
    Short Story in One Long Evening
7 Days and 11 Nights: Writing a
        Novella for the Digital Age
Devil's Lake
The Trouble with Happiness
Dancing in the Rain
Without a Blindfold
Playing Chess with My Daughter
Boarded Windows
Lorine Niedecker: Enough to Carry Me Through
Writing is My Religion

PLAYS
A Brief History of My Tattoo
The Jane Test
The Writer's Cave
Last Day of the Sixties
John Jumps
Shadows of Unseen Things

COMPACT DISKS
10 Things I Think I Know for Sure
    about Getting Your Writing Published
The Writer's Cave: Why Writers Write
    What They Do
How and Why a Poem Works
    & Stopping by the Woods

PRAISE FOR LEHMAN'S *SHORTS*

Lehman is the master of the telling last image or line, the kind that socks into place like a baseball hitting the sweet spot in a glove... The little hairs on the back of my neck stood up when I read "How I Learned to Drown," with its killer lines "...After the rescue he vowed he'd never / again go farther out than where he could touch / bottom. I'd rather drown than live by that philosophy..." I wanted to leap out of my desk chair and shout "Hallelujah!" — *Harriet Brown, Editor, Wisconsin Trails Magazine*

With *Shorts* Lehman gives us one of the marvelous possibilities of the prose poem: something of Midwestern American prose, something of the haiku, humor and high seriousness all in the space of five or six sentences! — *Louis Jenkins, Nice Fish: New and Selected Prose Poems*

John Lehman has more Wisconsin on his boots than any other writer I know. — *John Tuschen, Madison's First Poet Laureate*

Shorts: One-Hundred-And-One Brief Poems Of Wonder And Surprise is an eclectic anthology of the succinct poetry and imaginative prose of John Lehman. Organized as a "best-yet" collection of his poetry, *Shorts* offers his readers an "unseen insight" into an extraordinary mind and talent. A Chinese Puzzle: My first wife was artistic, self-assured and short: / the second, slender, more spontaneous and warm. / Perhaps at different ages I needed different things: / "young man, lacking confidence, seeks an articulate / voice" became "failing businessman desires a sweet / embrace." But, that's unfair to both. No, it's more like / someone eating take-out food by himself who's been / given two fortune cookies, instead of one. "You will / succeed beyond your wildest dreams says the first, while the other warns all things are subject to drastic / change. Does this mean I"ll find success and give it up because happiness is just a u-turn away? The answer is / as puzzling as two women, so different, who I've loved / or the sun shining in the rain. — *Midwest Book Review*

REVIEWS OF DOGS DREAM OF RUNNING

John Lehman is a dazzling poet with a shiny wit, glimmering compassion and hard-earned wisdom. He writes like a bird dog runs: with energy, a big heart and—that rare thing in poetry—pure joy. And when this poet stops to point, you can be assured that what he's found is a beautiful and valuable prize. — *Dean Bakopoulos, Wisconsin Academy Review*

John Lehman has a wizard's eye for the telling human detail and the rude pinprick, as well as the intricate ironies of the heart. *Dogs Dream of Running* sneaks up on you with its range and thoroughness of vision. — *Bob Wake, Culture Vulture*

Poems that abound in surprise and delight... Lehman makes sense of twenty-first-century America. Deftly, he tells truths that wake us up to what we'd miss, and to a few things only he could know. — *X.J. Kennedy, former editor of the Paris Review*

These poems are full of spunk and insight. But what I like best is that the collection itself creates a picture of our times that is fascinatingly entertaining. There are real life encounters with Orson Welles, John Updike and Robert Mitchum as well as such diverse subjects as "two-fisted advertising," Alzheimer's

disease, the teaching of high school English, film noir and even a trilogy on flying saucers. The poem "Nobody Recognizes Robert Mitchum in Vietnam" is the finest I have ever read on that conflict and the parody of writing workshops is laugh-out-loud funny. Even people who don't like poetry that much are going to enjoy the great storytelling of "Dogs Dream of Running." And for people who like poetry or teach it, this book is a must.
                 —Jim Sharping